Burt and His Bag of Dirt

Level 4+
Blue+

Helpful Hints for Reading at Home

The graphemes (written letters) and phonemes (units of sound) used throughout this series are aligned with Letters and Sounds. This offers a consistent approach to learning whether reading at home or in the classroom.

THIS BLUE+ BOOK BAND SERVES AS AN INTRODUCTION TO PHASE 5. EACH BOOK IN THIS BAND USES ALL PHONEMES LEARNED UP TO PHASE 4, WHILE INTRODUCING ONE PHASE 5 PHONEME. HERE IS A LIST OF PHONEMES FOR THIS PHASE, WITH THE NEW PHASE 5 PHONEME. AN EXAMPLE OF THE PRONUNCIATION CAN BE FOUND IN BRACKETS.

Phase 3			
j (jug)	v (van)	w (wet)	x (fox)
y (yellow)	z (zoo)	zz (buzz)	qu (quick)
ch (chip)	sh (shop)	th (thin/then)	ng (ring)
ai (rain)	ee (feet)	igh (night)	oa (boat)
oo (boot/look)	ar (farm)	or (for)	ur (hurt)
ow (cow)	oi (coin)	ear (dear)	air (fair)
ure (sure)	er (corner)		

New Phase 5 Phoneme	ir (bird, dirt, smirk)

HERE ARE SOME WORDS WHICH YOUR CHILD MAY FIND TRICKY.

Phase 4 Tricky Words			
said	were	have	there
like	little	so	one
do	when	some	out
come	what		

TOP TIPS FOR HELPING YOUR CHILD TO READ:

- Allow children time to break down unfamiliar words into units of sound and then encourage children to string these sounds together to create the word.

- Encourage your child to point out any focus phonics when they are used.

- Read through the book more than once to grow confidence.

- Ask simple questions about the text to assess understanding.

- Encourage children to use illustrations as prompts.

This book introduces the phoneme /ir/ and is a Blue+ Level 4+ book band.

Burt and His Bag of Dirt

Written by Robin Twiddy **Illustrated by** Drue Rintoul

"Sir, this is the best dirt," said Burt the bird with a smirk.

Burt got a bag of dirt from his pocket.
"Look. See? It is the best dirt!" said Burt.

"You need this dirt," Burt said to Otter as he hid his smirk.

Otter was firm.
"I do not need that dirt!" he said, and then he was off.

Burt went to see Lobster.
"Lobster will need the dirt," said Burt.

Lobster was asleep.
"A tap, tap, tap will disturb Lobster,"
said Burt.

"Tell me, Lobster. Do you wish to sing better?" said Burt.

"I do. If I was better at singing, I might be first in the singing contest," said Lobster.

"If you wish to be first, you will need my dirt. It is the best dirt," said Burt.

"I will sell it to you for ten coins," said Burt as he held up the bag of dirt.

"You must think I am thick. Dirt will not help me sing, sir!" said Lobster.

"I need an animal that is not clever and has a wish," said Burt. He went to look.

"There is Snail. I can tell what his wish is," said Burt. His smirk was back.

Burt must trick Snail to think that the dirt might get him a wish.

"Snail, have you seen my dirt?" said Burt. "It is the best dirt!"

"How is this the best dirt?" Burt said with a chirp.

"Let me tell you how this dirt is best," said Burt. He held up a wing to block his smirk.

"A little of this dirt on your shell and you will be as quick as me!" said Burt.

Snail had a plan to stop Burt from bothering the animals with his dirt.

"I cannot see well," Snail said to Burt. "Can you bring the dirt to that bright spot?"

"Near that fir tree," said Snail. Burt began to smirk.

"Will I be quick if this dirt is on my shell?" said Snail.

"Oh, so quick," said Burt with a smirk.
He began to rub his wings with glee.

"As quick as the wind?" said Snail with a smirk. "Let me see the dirt."

With a nod Burt held up the dirt.
Then there was a gust of wind.

The dirt began to twirl up and up on the wind. "That is quick," said Snail with a smirk.

Burt and His Bag of Dirt

1) What animals does Burt the bird try to sell his dirt to?

2) What was Lobster doing when Burt found her?

3) What did Lobster wish she could do better?

4) How many coins does Burt try to sell his dirt for?

5) How do you think Burt felt when he was tricked?

©2022 **BookLife Publishing Ltd.**
King's Lynn, Norfolk PE30 4LS

ISBN 978-1-80155-170-0

All rights reserved. Printed in Poland.
A catalogue record for this book is available from the British Library.

Burt and his Bag of Dirt
Written by Robin Twiddy
Illustrated by Drue Rintoul

An Introduction to BookLife Readers...

Our Readers have been specifically created in line with the London Institute of Education's approach to book banding and are phonetically decodable and ordered to support each phase of the Letters and Sounds document.

Each book has been created to provide the best possible reading and learning experience. Our aim is to share our love of books with children, providing both emerging readers and prolific page-turners with beautiful books that are guaranteed to provoke interest and learning, regardless of ability.

BOOK BAND GRADED using the Institute of Education's approach to levelling.

PHONETICALLY DECODABLE supporting each phase of Letters and Sounds.

EXERCISES AND QUESTIONS to offer reinforcement and to ascertain comprehension.

BEAUTIFULLY ILLUSTRATED to inspire and provoke engagement, providing a variety of styles for the reader to enjoy whilst reading through the series.

AUTHOR INSIGHT:
ROBIN TWIDDY

Robin Twiddy is one of BookLife Publishing's most creative and prolific editorial talents, who imbues all his copy with a sense of adventure and energy. Robin's Cambridge-based first class honours degree in psychosocial studies offers a unique viewpoint on factual information and allows him to relay information in a manner that readers of any age are guaranteed to retain. He also holds a certificate in Teaching in the Lifelong Sector, and a postgraduate certificate in Consumer Psychology.

A father of two, Robin has written over 70 titles for BookLife and specialises in conceptual, role-playing narratives which promote interaction with the reader and inspire even the most reluctant of readers to fully engage with his books.

This book introduces the phoneme /ir/ and is a Blue+ Level 4+ book band.